Te

A Widow's Journey

How I Went From Loss to Learning to Moving on

"Bea Lewis' sincere and heartwarming telling of her personal experiences, starting with the death of her husband of 50 years, and her three year journey from abject despondency and the significant challenges of widowhood, ending with acceptance and discovery of her inner resources to finally "get a life," is a testament to the resiliency of the human spirit. Bea does not pull any punches as she describes the caregiver stress her husband's deteriorating health had on her and her sadness and loneliness after he died.

She describes with candor and humor all she had to learn to become independent, as well as with the ups and downs, disappointments and frustrations of being single. Although one can never fully emotionally prepare for the death of a husband, I believe that the lessons from Bea's journey need to be learned before a woman is widowed, as a prophylactic measure to lessen the potential devastating consequences of loss, and to appreciate that a meaningful chapter of one's life is possible – even as one occasionally continues to mourn and feel sad."

Bert Diament, Ph.D., licensed psychologist
Faculty Florida Atlantic University Lifelong Learning
Private practice Boynton Beach, Fl.

A must-read for adult children who have lost a parent. While coping with your own grief, this book can help you gain a better understanding of – and to be more compassionate about – what your widowed mom or dad is going through.

Laurie Feldman, MSW, Virginia Beach, Va.

Bea's personal journey from widowhood to a new and fulfilling life is inspirational and will give comfort to those traveling the same path.

Ann Bair LCSW, Boca Raton, FL.

Bea's writing is authentic…her essays move me in a deep emotional way… moving and inspiring...

Joseph J. Bernadino, Col.,USAF (ret.)

Praise for Bea Lewis' – *My Kids Are All Grown Up, So Why Are They Still Driving Me Crazy* – and Lewis' speaking engagements:

"…popular speaker at the ACE Lifelong Learning Center at the Mandel JCC in Boynton Beach…her skills at communicating and relating to others are exceptional."

Alan Egenthal, director ACE Lifelong Learning Center.

"… we were mesmerized for over an hour with her inspiring and practical suggestions."

Jacquie Fox, Platina Singles Group.

"A superbly entertaining and informative speaker…her topics about daughters-in-law issues, mixed marriages, money issues, grandchild/grandparent problems, facing disappointments and more - were handled with humor and common sense.

Vera Rekstad, Women's Group at The Club at Indian Lakes.

"…glad to have you back…we've received positive feedback from your last talk."

Gessy Volcimus, Palm Beach County Library system.

"…good feeling to know that we are not alone in dealing with so many family issues….feedback was most positive…"

Claire Kalman, Bellagio PAP Corp chapter

"It's no mystery why Bea Lewis is in great demand as a speaker…"

Ruth Sabo, Ora Delray Hadassah

"Bea kept 150 women totally engrossed (and quiet) for the entire program!"

Freda Golden, Cascades Women's Club

"Our group is still talking about your presentation…. wonderful, informative program…"

Marsha Gruder, Aberdeen East Snowbird Club

A Widow's Journey

How I Went From Loss to Learning to Moving on

BEA LEWIS

With Marilyn Murray Willison

Previous works:

My Kids Are All Grown Up, So Why Are They Still Driving Me Crazy?: How To Get Along With Your Adult Children, Their Spouses and Other Aliens

Website:
http://bealewis.com

Amazon Author Page:
https://www.amazon.com/author/bealewis

ISBN-13: 978-1537256757
ISBN-10: 1537256750

CONTENTS

INTRODUCTION

It's no secret that life has many chapters and many transitions. That's why, through the years, we all find ourselves moving from one phase to another. In my case, I left childhood, entered adolescence, and before I knew it, I graduated college, began teaching in elementary school, and then met the man of my dreams. And when I married Edwin Lewis, I took on a completely new identity—the one known as "Wife."

During our 50 years together, we had three daughters who grew up, married and gave us six beautiful grandchildren. Truth be told, during our five decades of marriage, my late husband and I had our share of ups and downs. There were heart attacks (which Ed survived), the open heart surgery that almost claimed his life, as well as the spinal cord injury that left him disabled and unable to walk. The years brought a laundry list of health complications and disabilities until—in his later years— Ed was totally unable to care for himself.

During our marriage, I suffered from chronic bouts of clinical depression, which created tsunamis of sadness for

Ed—as well as an overdose of confusion for our daughters. Plus—as happens in so many marriages—there were plenty of financial and in-law issues that created a number of stressful episodes during our many years together.

Fortunately, there was also a warm and loving abundance of wonderful memories as well. Maybe even a surplus of them, which is probably what helped to keep our marriage together. Today, years later, I treasure the fun times our family had together, as well as the care and support we always managed to offer each other. The love and pride that Ed and I shared for all three of our daughters was so intense that it would be impossible to imagine our lives without their presence.

But then, suddenly, I entered a new chapter of my life—Widowhood—that came with a new (unwanted) label. I've learned that this transition, however, unlike those of earlier years, has no guidelines and no paths to follow—it's just an open field with way too many thorns and bramble bushes along the way. That phase is addressed in the LOSS section of this book.

In the early months after Ed died, I (literally) didn't have a single clue about which way to turn or what direction to seek. I certainly didn't know what I would want to do with the rest of my life because I honestly had no idea of who I was without a husband by my side.

The loneliness I felt at nighttime was a killer, and finances—which Ed had always handled—now became my burden. Some of the close friendships we'd had as a couple slipped away, and now that I was a single woman (sadly) several were no longer a functioning part of my life.

My daughters had been extraordinarily attentive and caring to Ed while he was ill, but they—understandably—

returned to their own lives and families after he died. I sorely missed how supportive they'd been with me during their father's decline, but I knew that I needed to—and I had to—let them focus on their more immediate personal concerns. It was time for me to learn how to stand on my own two feet. As their mother, the thought of ever being a lonely, broken burden to them was nothing less than totally abhorrent.

During those first few years as a widow, I gradually learned to call upon the coping tools I'd developed earlier in order to help me figure out three important things: Who I was, what I wanted, and how I would live out the remaining years of my life. That phase is addressed in the LEARNING section of this book.

Eventually, thousands—it seemed like countless—lonely hours prompted me to consider (as I weighted the pros and cons of being someone's significant other) the awkward issue of late-life romantic companionship. Soon I made the brave decision to begin dating to explore (and learn first-hand) what I would want—or need—from an intimate relationship. And I learned that—as the expression goes—you have to kiss a lot of frogs before you find your prince.

Perhaps the most important realization I made after Ed's death was that I needed to find out what would bring joy back into my life. What would help me to wake up every morning, be comfortable in my own skin, and be happy to greet another day? You will learn about this phase in the MOVING ON section of this book.

On the following pages, I share the good, the bad, the ugly (as well as the humorous) aspects of both my challenging journey, and my transition to the new me. I cordially invite you to share my evolution from Mrs.

Edwin Lewis to Ms. Bea Lewis—the finally fulfilled, most happy, and peaceful person I can be.

LOSS

The song is ended...but the memory lingers on...

Irving Berlin

The Final Years

Ed had a deteriorating illness that included severe stenosis, scoliosis and neuropathy, but what finally killed him was yet another—and final—bout of congestive heart failure. For years, Ed had tried to undergo surgery to relieve his horrific back pain and increasing inability to walk by himself. But because of his heart issues, it was simply not "in the cards."

During Ed's last five or so years, he "progressed" from using a cane, to relying on a walker, and then being confined to a wheelchair. Little by little, he became totally dependent on me and others for his basic needs. And this meant that our world as once active Florida retirees became more restricted. Gone were the days when we would loll on the beach. The outdoor concerts on breezy warm evenings became mere memories. There was no way I could help (i.e. physically lift) him in and out of our car. Eating meals together in restaurants also became off limits because Ed could no longer cut his food or hold a cup or glass without spilling its contents.

Instead, his last few years were filled with falls, infections, bed sores, painful neuropathy, and numerous bouts of heart failure that sent us racing to the emergency room more times than I can remember. Checking in and out of hospitals became a constant activity in our lives.

During his last year, this once strapping, handsome, suntanned, strong-bodied husband of mine became so impaired that it took two people (usually me and a paid caregiver) to lift him in and out of bed or to position him on the toilet. The personal sense of humiliation that he felt was more than he could bear and—not surprisingly— he turned his anger against me. "Damn it," he would rage. "I can take care of myself. Just give me time to get on the f.... toilet seat and stay out of here." At first, I followed his angry orders and stood guard outside the bathroom. But when Ed's ego-centric and unrealistic sense of independence got the best of him, I knew I had to take back control of his care.

Once when I was standing outside the bathroom, I heard Ed let out a piercing scream that was followed by a loud smash. He had tried to get off the toilet by himself, but had lost his balance, and toppled over. His head had hit the cold (and truly rock-solid) tile floor. His insistent request for bathroom privacy would no longer be honored.

To this day, I often feel guilty about my behavior, which ranged from clenching my fists in anger to fantasizing about smacking him when he was verbally abusive to me. When caring for him left me forlorn and exhausted, I would scream louder than I ever thought possible. And only when my voice became so hoarse that I could hardly talk would I realize that those shrieks were coming from a buried place deep down inside of me.

One time, after Ed had fallen, my screams were so loud that within minutes my next door neighbor, Phyllis was at my side, rubbing my back, and speaking to me in a whisper. Her calming tone was unruffled and demure. I could hardly hear her, because of the blaring siren of the Palm Beach County Rescue squad, which was coming closer to my house. The fire truck stopped in front, and four strong paramedics came to our aid. They lifted Ed off the bathroom floor, strapped him onto the gurney, attached oxygen to his nostrils, and drove him to the nearby emergency room. That time Ed was lucky—tests showed no concussion, but his face and arms were badly bruised.

Later, as I sat by his side in that emergency room, I was relieved that he was not in danger. It was just another one of the many mishaps he would continue to experience as his body became progressively weaker.

As my anger and fear began to subside, I started to cry out of gratitude that he was okay. I felt so sorry for him, and wondered what the hell did I want or expect from this helpless suffering man?

And in that moment, I only felt love and compassion for my sweet struggling husband. The rage I'd felt for the burden placed upon my shoulders began to dissipate, and I promised myself to try and be more patient. Still, the burden of caring for Ed remained both physically and emotionally overwhelming.

As his health continued to decline, my life became fully focused on his care and his needs. Because of my role as Ed's fulltime caregiver, I felt—like a bear in the woods that had gotten his foot stuck in a metal trap— unable to go anywhere or do anything that didn't revolve around my husband's illness.

But soon things actually began to get better—if not with his health, then at least with our relationship. A week after the hospital trek to check for a concussion (and/or other problems)—during a visit to his doctor's office, the doctor suggested that we consider having more help in the house. Turning to me, he added, "And Bea, I worry about you, too. If you don't get help, I will have both of you as patients."

He was right. Each new day brought new stressful physical challenges and I wondered, "How long can this continue?" Enter Malinder, our Jamaican hired aide, who not only helped Ed cheerfully with the chores of daily living, but also gave me the confidence that Ed was in safe, experienced hands.

For most of Ed's last few months, heavy-duty medications kept his pain at bay. But the downside of taking those drugs was that they caused his mind to lose thoughts. He lost the ability to finish a sentence. He tried to remember what he wanted to say, but very little would come out. This pattern grew more and more noticeable, and after a while, Ed became less and less talkative, because he was afraid he would—and he did forget what he wanted to say. Ever so slowly, Ed began to accept his need for help. He eventually stopped fighting so furiously for his "independence," and let me help him with even the most intimidating personal chores.

Ironically, the less he fought me, the more kindness and compassion I felt. It became so much easier to give him the loving and patient care he needed so badly.

Fortunately, this change came in enough time for both of us to fully embrace and appreciate each other. The more he accepted his situation, the more he would express gratitude for how I would help him. Ed's affection increased tenfold. He never let me walk past his wheelchair without reaching out to hug or kiss me—and I was more than happy to return these warm and demonstrative caresses.

For the first time in years, I felt truly loved. I—finally—had no doubt about the important and irreplaceable role I had played in Ed's final years.

The Last Days

When everything became a struggle for Ed, when he slept most of the day and eating was no longer of interest, the doctors told me that the end was near. They suggested that I consider calling in Hospice, the organization that helps people cope with their last days on earth. While some hospice patients are kept in the hospital, I insisted that Ed should pass away at home.

My three daughters and the older grandchildren spent the last few days with me, helping to make Ed as comfortable as could be. When Ed could no longer speak, the Hospice nurses assured us that Ed could still hear us. And so we reminded him about the days when he played beauty parlor with the granddaughters and barber shop with Josh. When he could no longer eat or drink, we were told to keep his mouth moist with water-soaked sponges. Laurie, knowing how much he loved egg creams, the Bronx drink of his childhood, wiped his parched lips with a few drops of the blend of chocolate syrup, milk and seltzer. We thought—and hoped—we saw him smile. We played his favorite symphonic music, especially The *Moldau* by Bedrich Smetana. Long before I was ready, the hospice nurses, who knew when the end was near, encouraged us to say our goodbyes. I was speechless. Jen however, stepped up to the plate.

"You don't have to be in pain anymore, daddy. We will remember you always." And then, as Jen gave him the signal that it was OK to leave us, Ed took his last breath. Calmly, easily. Without a struggle. It was the moment, just as the sun set in the sky and at the beginning of the Sabbath that I became a widow and our daughters became fatherless. Ed had entered a place of peace, where, at some point in the future, I hope to be with him again.

I will always be grateful that during his long illness, Ed and I found our way to (finally) put into practice the marriage vow we'd made some 50 years earlier—the one where we promised to stick together in sickness and in health. After a long, arduous struggle, my Ed died peacefully, taking his last breaths in the bed we slept in, made love in, conceived our three daughters in, and where—during countless hours of late-night pillow talk— we'd discussed all the ways we would grow old together.

The Funeral
"Your kind expression of sympathy is gratefully acknowledged and deeply appreciated"

Dearest Ed,

I wish you could have been at your funeral, and seen all the people who came to say their goodbyes. The chapel was standing-room only. People came from as far away as California and Texas, and even friends you grew up with (and with whom you kept in contact until the end) flew in to say their goodbyes.

When our daughters and grandson, Josh, gave the eulogies, there literally was not a dry eye in the chapel. I could hear sniffling from the very last rows.

Laurie told of the days when you marched on Washington with thousands of others to protest the U.S. involvement in the Vietnam War, and how proud she was that her "Daddy" walked the walk, not just talked the talk.

She told how you both got hooked on the popular TV show, *Breaking Bad*, which aired Sunday nights. Even toward the end, when it was difficult for you to speak or remember, she told how you struggled to keep up with your morning after telephone discussions.

Jen said that you had been a man of determination. "He was dogged. He was a fighter—not as a wartime soldier, but as a maker of peace—an agent of change for justice, for righteousness and equality."

Kimberly spoke of her childhood. "My dad wore a coat of many colors," she began. "He was our caretaker—he kissed our booboos when we got hurt, and when we were sick he would mash the baby aspirin in water to make it easier for us to swallow. He was a steady ender in our jump rope games.

He was our tour guide—taking us on road trips to Civil War sites and other historical places. He was our protector. My dad kept a baseball bat in the trunk of his car, and I'm sure it wasn't to play baseball, but to make sure no one ever messed with his family!"

Then came Josh. "I'm the only boy grandchild; that's why papa called me the Prince." His comment brought ripples of laughter.

The speech he gave "blew everyone out of the park" with his vivid description of a hot day in the playground, when he was about four-years old. "Papa would push me on the swing—back and forth, back and forth—even when his arms grew tired and sweat dripped down his face. He told me that he would always have my back, and although I didn't understand it at the time, Papa was the one, all my life, who I could turn to—especially when I needed help solving a problem. Rest in peace, Papa," he said, holding back his tears.

Oh, Ed, you were such a nurturing father. Looking back, I realize that you were ahead of your time—like today's dads who change baby diapers and share child-rearing and household responsibilities.

And when an opportunity arose for me to be hired as

a staff writer for *Newsday*—a major New York newspaper—you were my cheerleader, encouraging me to become the person I had always dreamed about. Not too many husbands of that generation would allow themselves to become the "man behind the woman."

Donations in your honor sent to the Boynton Beach Soup Kitchen (where you volunteered as a Friday cook) were too numerous to count. Even when you struggled to walk, you still got up at 4 am to prepare the soups, meatloaf and chicken dishes for the indigent.

When we got home from your funeral, the dining room table overflowed with platters of food that friends had delivered for the *Shiva (Jewish mourning period.)* That night, and for days afterwards, friends and more friends came to pay their condolences. It was heartwarming to have so much support. But looking back, our daughters and I were in a fog, going through the motions of saying "Thank you for coming," and accepting big hugs as our friends left with promises to keep in touch. While some did, others never called or visited again.

When the friends and neighbors left, the girls and I—exhausted and feeling numb—sat quietly in the living room with our shoes off, and feet propped up on the coffee table. We talked about how difficult it will be to face life without you. But then I remembered something I had read long ago.

When we lose someone we love, we must learn not to live without them, but to live with the love they left behind.

And dearest Ed, I truly believe that you have left us with more than enough love to carry us through for a lifetime. Rest in peace.

All my love,

Bea

Reality Sets In

It was early evening when the crimson red Florida sunset faded into darkness and the last of my family members hugged me goodbye. The seven day *Shiva (Jewish mourning period)* was over and I knew my children needed to get on with their lives. But I still felt abandoned. It was the same scary numbness I'd felt when, at the age of six, my father told me that my mother had died. Now—seventy years later—my first instinct was to run outside to my family, and beg them to please come back.

But I knew that I shouldn't be selfish—so I bravely resisted the temptation to chase them down. Then, alone in the darkness of the living room, I cried to make up for months of holding myself together while Ed was falling apart. The only light came from the memorial candle that the funeral home had given us to remember our beloved. Rabbis tell us that the flame—which brings light into the world—is compared to a person's soul.

When there were no tears left, I turned on the lights and looked at myself in the mirror. My hair was a mess, my mascara had spread all over my face from crying, and it was obvious that I was still in shock.

The bitter truth was that there was no more Ed for me to talk to, make love with, be a wife and companion to, or even act as an ever-vigilant caregiver-in-chief.

It seemed clear to me that the only way to relieve my anguish was simply to go to sleep, even though (for most people) it was barely dinnertime. As I crawled into bed, I yanked the recently-purchased comforter over my head. (Our old one had been thrown out because it had blood stains from a fall Ed had taken days before.)

The bed that Ed and I had shared for half a century was now half empty. I had a flashback to when, only a few weeks earlier, his oxygen tubes had dislodged whenever we'd tried to embrace each other.

My first nights were horribly—painfully—lonely, but the TV reruns of *Everyone Loves Raymond* kept me company. I slept on and off until the telephone awakened me early one morning. *Damn it, I'm finally able to get some decent sleep, and now some idiot calls trying to sell me some life insurance.* And although I think I was still in shock, I knew it was time for me to get up and face reality.

I stumbled into the kitchen to reheat a cup of stale coffee, turned on *The Today Show*, and watched the breaking news about the tornadoes in the Midwest. I felt sorry for the people who had lost so much, but—honestly—I cared more about my own loss. The longer I watched, though, the more I was amazed at the strength of those sturdy Mid-western survivors. Totally devastated by those freakish storms, they had somehow been able to resolutely put their lives back together. Their quiet courage inspired me to get up, shower (for the first time in days), get dressed, and do my best to look like a (relatively normal) human being.

I then opened the front door for the first time since

my family had left, and welcomed in a new day. For one foolish moment, I believed that my sorrow had passed, and my grieving was over.

Little did I know what lay ahead.

The Bereavement Group

A few months after Ed died, I signed up for a 12-week support group for widows and widowers that was to be held at a local synagogue. We were ten women, two men, and a social worker who would facilitate the meetings. We all sat in a semi-circle in that small, stuffy room, and for the first few weeks I listened to the men, who talked about feeling totally helpless. One of them—who wore a rumpled shirt and stained shorts—said that he still couldn't figure out how to use the washing machine. The other, a tall, slender man with a slight pot belly, nodded in agreement, and then he admitted to eating Total cereal for dinner most nights.

By the fifth week, one of the two widowers began sharing stories about the three widowed ladies he was dating. I was bored and restless, but listened to him tell us about the fabulous dinners (brisket with all the side dishes) they cooked for him, and the leftovers stacked in his freezer. "All the weight I lost after my wife died," he said with a smile, "I am now gaining back." He laughed as he rubbed his stomach.

The other grieving widower also seemed to be getting on—rather quickly—with his life. He was now wearing a pair of stylish Tommy Bahama shorts, and also boasted that the belt on his shorts was a notch tighter. "Pretty ladies don't like men with bellies," was a comment that got all of us laughing. His neighbor, he said, had taken him shopping, and he now had a whole collection of classy, color-coordinated new clothes hanging in his closet.

"Wow, it sounds like you have a great neighbor," said the blonde lady with the not-so-stylish bouffant hair-do who was sitting to his right.

"Yes, she is," he responded with a shy smile. "That figures," whispered the heavy-set woman to the widow in the next chair, who was also smirking.

When it came to taking care of their personal needs, it seemed that the women in our group fared much better than the men. But rather than talk about what they could or couldn't do, they cried a lot during those first few meetings—especially about how to go on with their lives as "a solo." Sharing their emotional anguish made our skinny counselor's eyes twitch, and her hand would swiftly pass the box of Kleenex to the sobbing women.

But soon the women moved beyond the logistics of living alone, and began to share their relationship stories. Bertha (not her real name) told how she was "off men forever," after just having buried her third husband. Carole, on the other hand, couldn't get past the guilt she felt in connection to her husband's death. "His stomach pains kept getting worse, and although we went from doctor to doctor, no one seemed to get a handle on the problem. Then…just before he died, my poor husband was diagnosed with end-stage stomach cancer. As her tears began to flow, she told the group that she felt so guilty for not taking him straight to New York. She felt that they should have sought the expertise of doctors at

Sloan Kettering, which she considered to be the world's best cancer center.

Our bereavement counselor asked her whether going to New York and getting the exact same diagnosis would have made her feel any less guilty. Before Carole could even answer, our social worker went on to explain that when a loved one dies—especially one who was in our care—the caregiver is always left with a feeling of, "Maybe I didn't do enough. But," she said, "None of us—no one in this room, or anywhere in the world—is powerful enough to save a loved one when there is nothing left to save. In your case," she added, pointing to Carole, "your husband's symptoms did not appear until his cancer was already near the end zone."

It took a few more sessions with the counselor for Carole to accept that she had done all that she could. Only after doing that would Carole be able to get on with her life. The following week, Carole told us that she had gone back to playing tennis, and asked if we liked her new stylish hairdo. She was now a blonde, she said, "because I hear that blondes have more fun!"

Denial is Not a River in Egypt

I was beginning to feel like an oddball. The recently widowed friends and acquaintances that I knew all seemed lost in their grief. A few friends were still clinging to their beloved's clothing and belongings. One friend even went so far as to go to bed each night holding tightly onto her deceased husband's shirts.

Friends were asking what they could do to help ease my pain. Feeling confused, I thought to myself, "What pain?" Looking back, I wonder if perhaps I was just numb or maybe even stuck in a state of shock. I wasn't lying when I told them, *"I am doing just fine."*

Why didn't I feel the type of excruciating "hold onto to the past" anguish that other women said they felt after their spouses' death? To be honest, the first few months after Ed died, I actually felt relieved that he was finally out of pain, and I was free of my care-giving responsibilities. An experience like that is gruesome not only for the ill spouse, but also for the care-giving mate who is forced to watch someone they love so deeply slide slowly downhill. Ed's eventual death was—for me—like being granted an inexorable stay of execution, I was—at last—free of the heart-wrenching chore of giving him round-the-clock care.

Experts tell us that grieving has no timetable, and that grief is as unique as a fingerprint. But what I learned from reading about the different stages (anger, denial, depression, acceptance), is that I stayed stuck in denial for far too long. It was a way to protect myself from having to deal with the deep genuine pain of my loss. But how long can you hold onto that fragile tree branch before it snaps, and you find yourself flat on the ground?

It took from June—when Ed died—until November for the reality of his "gone forever, never coming back" to hit me.

I was spending the Thanksgiving holiday weekend at my daughter Kimberly's home with my children and grandchildren, waiting for the platter of turkey and its trimmings to be passed around. As I looked around the table, I suddenly realized that Ed wasn't there. There was one less chair at the table, as well as one fewer plate, set of silver, and wine glass. My Ed was gone, and he wouldn't ever be back.

When I began to feel—really feel—the pain of losing Ed, it was, as the kids would say, "OMG—this is so excruciating." It was at that moment that I began to grieve deeply for my beloved husband. I needed to find relief. Even though it was months after the fact, my daughter Laurie who is a trained social worker, suggested that I make an appointment with a licensed, experienced bereavement counselor. I felt I was ready to face the future, but I didn't want to face it alone.

Truth be told, it was one of the best decisions I made. I knew I needed help to get back into my life—and to even begin trying to move forward.

Ed Reappears at Passover

My first Passover without Ed was just around the corner. I had heard from others, but never really believed it, that the spirit of the deceased loved ones come back to us at odd times, or at least when thoughts of them are totally unexpected.

Weeks before what would be my first Passover without Ed, I found myself lost in thought about what the traditional meal would be like without Ed seated at the head of the table. One night, around 4 am, the sound of a large THUD woke me up from what I thought was one of those true-to-life dreams. But this racket was not a part of a dream; this crash was for real.

On the wall, just to the right side of my bed, a large heavily framed 15X17 picture of the Milan Opera House had fallen onto the uncarpeted area of our bedroom. With my heart pounding, I jumped out of bed to investigate, but saw nothing amiss. The hooks were where they should be, as was the wire that had kept the picture hanging securely on the wall for years.

Our Passover Seders had always been "Ed's thing." For 50 years, I did the cooking and food preparations, and it was Ed's job to conduct the services—not only for the family, but for many of our friends as well. Each year, his sermons and explanations of the holiday became more detailed, and more meaningful. And—oh, yes—the services grew longer and more detailed each year. (Yawn.)

Getting back to the fallen picture. When I got back in bed—only to toss and turn—I tried to understand what had just happened. I eventually realized that Ed had given me a signal. But what was he saying? Then it came to me, clear as the ring from a crystal goblet glass when it's tapped.

Ed really wanted to be remembered—and be missed—at our Passover Seder. Just as I had always set the table with his plate at the then head, I am sure that was what he expected me to do again this year.

When I shared my "insight," no one thought it was a crazy idea. In fact, my daughters were delighted. The younger grandchildren, however, were a bit spooked just as their mothers had been when they were little and Ed would put a filled glass of wine in the middle of the table for the prophet Elijah, and somehow by the end of the evening that glass was almost empty.

And so the message sent by the fallen picture was clear. Ed's spirit would be with us throughout the holiday to remind us of the lessons he'd taught all of us for decades while we sat around the Seder table. Ed's place was set—again, and as always—at the head of the table. We couldn't see him with our eyes, but we definitely felt his presence with our hearts.

Sex and the Single Girl

He reached over to my side of our extra large king-sized-bed. As he wrapped his arm around my body, he pressed his hand against my right breast, and made tiny gentle circles around my nipple. I moaned softly as my body hungrily responded to his touch. Ed always knew exactly how to ignite my passion. As he reached down to press his hand between my thighs, I turned onto my back, and hastily pulled my black lace nightgown upward so he could climb atop my naked body. My excitement mounted, and having him so close to me quickly resulted in a satisfying orgasm, a feeling I hadn't had in such a long time.

"Oh, that was heavenly," I said, inhaling deeply as my body continued to inwardly vibrate from the amazing sexual encounter I had just experienced. "It's been so long, Ed, where have you been?"

I thought about the last time we had tried to make love. Ed's oxygen tubes had dislodged and we'd been forced to stop, which had left us both feeling frustrated and demoralized. Our time for lovemaking had been erased; Ed's need to breathe became the priority.

"But this time, Ed, You're breathing so easily without

the oxygen tubes. And look, you are actually out of pain." Ed didn't answer, but when he kissed me softly on the back of my neck, it felt heavenly.

And then suddenly—without warning—that glorious moment in time, and that warm loving feeling, just faded away. And so did Ed.

I woke up startled. My heart was beating so fast that I felt it would explode. My nightgown was drenched in sweat. When I reached over to Ed's side of the bed, the sheet was cool and the pillow was untouched. There was only an empty space where I had dreamt that Ed had just brought me so much physical pleasure.

The clock on the side of my bed kept ticking away, the ceiling fan above my bed continued to whirl around quietly. A hint of light that began to show through the half-closed blinds signaled that it was almost morning.

I quickly got out of bed, anxious to be fully awake. I needed to slow down my pounding heart, and calm my frazzled nerves. "Damn it, Ed. How could you do this to me," I angrily asked the empty bed. And for the longest time I sat all alone in that room; not another person on the planet knew what my body and soul had experienced.

I didn't want to go back to sleep, and relive the aching anguish of my loss. So instead, I moved to a bedside chair and wrapped a blanket around my shivering body. I reached for the pillow that used to lie on Ed's side of the bed and buried my face into it. I loved the lingering smell of his Ralph Lauren aftershave lotion. Slowly, my confused anger turned to sadness and the bereavement tears began streaming down my face.

Having him to love me and hold me in a dream was no bargain, because when he faded away, I was even lonelier than before.

In one of the bereavement classes I'd attended shortly

after Ed passed away, the leader had told us that it takes time to fully accept the death of a loved one.

But why was I having these extreme erotic dreams? It almost seemed as if God was teasing me, "Hahaha, have a little taste of a cherished memory, my dear. Just a little nibble, and then that glorious moment will again be gone."

I then remembered that I'd once read something in a book about grieving. The author explained that the partner left behind slowly forgets the physical aspects and traits of his or her loved one, but memories remain ours to retrieve whenever we want. It didn't make sense at the time, but so many painful months later, I finally got it.

Today, I know that dreams about Ed can help me revisit his warmth and love and, yes, even the exciting passion we used to share whenever I need to recapture the things I treasured about our relationship. In my dreams, fantasies can come true.

The Unveiling

It was almost a year since Ed had passed away, and I thought for sure that I was past the grieving stage. After all, I had made new friends, as well as gone out to the movies, dinners and shows.

So why was I experiencing an inexplicable funk? For days on end, I hardly left the house, overdosed on chocolate candies, and slept way—way—too much. I began to suspect that I was in the beginning stages of a serious illness.

When I went to see my primary care physician (Dr. David Felker), he assured me that (physically) I was absolutely fine. But then he asked if—possibly—I'd been feeling depressed lately.

"No, no," I answered. "I just can't seem to get myself moving. I had made plans to travel out of state this summer, but I've been worried that I might be seriously ill."

"Remind me," he asked. "How long ago did Ed pass away?"

"Almost a year ago," I told him. "The unveiling is this Sunday."

"That's it," he said. "Unveilings often give the loved

ones a feeling of closure. But Bea, in your case, I think you may be struggling with that. After 50 years of marriage, I don't blame you for not feeling ready to let go. But it's important to remember that Ed is in a better place. And now it's time for you to get on with your life.

"Are you my medical doctor," I joked, "or my psychiatrist?"

"Well, Bea, I'm both," he laughed. And then—as a warm and caring gesture—he gently placed his hand on my shoulder.

Could he be right? I wondered. I mentioned this "unveiling issue" to a friend whose husband had died a few years earlier. "Honey," she said, "You are still grieving—and those feelings will come when you least expect it.

You might be driving in the car, happy as can be, when all of a sudden you hear a romantic song that you and Ed loved. That's when—boom—out of nowhere— that powerful ache in your heart will rise up, and your tears will begin to flow.

"My suggestion," she said, "is to allow yourself to feel the loss, and then let it go."

"Like meditation," I laughed. "Breathe in, breathe out, breathe in, breathe out."

"Exactly," she agreed. "As it comes, so will you let it go."

After I learned I didn't have that imaginary illness, our family gathered at a Miami cemetery to pay homage to Grandpa's final resting place.

My daughter, Laurie, explained the significance of this event to the younger children in the family by saying, "An unveiling is a Jewish custom that dates back to the book of Genesis. According to the time-honored story, the grieving Jacob set a pillar to mark the final resting place of his beloved wife, Rachel," she told them.

"First, we will say prayers for Grandpa," she added, "and then each of us will share a loving memory."

Julia, who is in graduate school, spoke first. "Whenever he would hug me, I could smell Grandpa's Ralph Lauren aftershave lotion. And I still can."

Ella, the youngest grandchild, remembered how Papa laughed whenever she came up with silly names for him – like "popcorn" or "Popsicle." And Hannah told how— when she was little, Grandpa was the first person who would be awake to prepare her favorite breakfast—ice cream and potato chips!

As we walked away from Ed's burial place, my son-in-law, Marc, pointed to the inscription on a nearby gravesite.

Etched lettering on the marble monument announced that the deceased man had "GONE FISHING!" *Hmmm*, I thought. *Maybe that's the kind of "better place" scenario that Dr. Felker wanted me to understand.* I was trying hard to accept that wherever Ed was, he was probably smiling. And that meant it was finally time for me to ditch (a) the marathon sleeping sessions, (b) the excess chocolate, and (c) the non-productive crying jags.

As we walked back to the car, Ella reached for my hand, looked up at me, and in her sweet and kind ten-year-old voice, whispered, "Grandma, I love you."

Obviously, it was also time to put a smile on my face as well.

The Anniversary Blues

It was one of those days when I was really feeling down in the dumps. I just couldn't get myself going. All I wanted to do was get back into bed, pull the covers over my head, and pretend this day never happened.

What's bothering me? Why am I so blue? And then—when I looked at my cell phone—I saw that it was June 30th. Bingo! I realized it was the date when—over 53 years ago—Ed and I were married.

Suddenly, I really missed Ed more than I had in the last few months, and—suddenly—I wished he were still here, which was a feeling I hadn't had in a long time. I had been moving on, and learning to live on my own. I was pretty pleased with how well I was orchestrating my life as a solo. *So why did I have this setback?*

Experts tell us that grief is a commodity that has no expiration date. And the pain associated with a severe loss can come galloping round the corner when you least expect it. According to what I have read about the grieving process, that pang in your gut is on speed dial whenever you are faced with special events such as a holiday, birthday, or—as it was in my case—an anniversary.

It's no secret that these "triggers" can reawaken memories and feelings that have been buried deeply within the recesses of our minds because they are too painful to even think about. They are, however, a lot easier to cope with if you prepare yourself ahead of time for these emotional wallops.

A good friend—who had become a widow a few years before I did—told me that she marks her calendar with the dates that she thinks will stir up memories that (because they are past tense) will cause her to be very, very sad. So she diligently plans to do something pleasant that will distract her—things like going to a play with a friend or basking in the beautiful paintings at her local art museum.

But I felt—intuitively—that her distraction tactic wouldn't work for me. Instead, I wanted to fully remember and embrace that very special day in my life— the magical time when Ed and I said our vows under a floral *chupa* at a very fancy hotel in New York City. I really wanted to remember how glorious I felt in a sequin-covered floor-length off-white wedding gown with a long flowing veil. At the time, I wasn't happy that I'd had to borrow the ensemble from a friend who'd been married a few months before my special day because I couldn't afford to buy my own dress. But I was really thrilled to look like so many of the bridal magazine models that I had admired ever since Ed and I had become engaged.

As I reminisced about that long-ago day, I could feel the warmth and affection that Ed had given me. He'd assured me that we were making the right move, and he promised that everything would be wonderful. Ed was such a comfort to my craziness, and thinking about that now, I realize that he had served as my support system during so many of the important times of my life.

I wanted a more visual memory of that day, so I took our wedding album out from the back of our bedroom closet. I sat for at least an hour trying to absorb everything about that night, especially how handsome Ed looked, and—OMG—how very young we'd been.

As I turned the pages, I recalled the silly poses we'd made, which were popular with wedding photographers of that era. You know the photo where the groom feeds the bride a large slice of the wedding cake, or where the newlyweds pose standing by a half-closed door with a sign that says, "Do Not Disturb."

The photo of my father escorting me down the aisle doesn't show that my hands were shaking or that they were moist and clammy from nerves. But the picture where Ed's parents—one on each side of him—walked him down the aisle looked as if they had been holding him up for dear life.

I remembered the moment when the Rabbi said, "I now pronounce you man and wife," and then that big wonderful kiss, and Ed's strong embrace. The memory of our friends and family as they cheered when the service was over—and we were now officially married—came back to me without pain and sorrow, but with a feeling of warmth and joy.

Part of what my journey has taught me is that a memory can rekindle happiness and joyful moments just as easily as it can create sorrow. Rather than concentrate on the loss, I chose to focus on one of the most wonderful days of my life.

But even if I had only spent our anniversary date crying over my loss, I know that my sorrow had been well earned. As Great Britain's Queen Elisabeth had once said, *"Grief is the price you pay for having loved."*

BEA LEWIS

42

LEARNING

Grief is in two parts. The first is loss—
the second is the remaking of life.

Anne Roiphe

My Trip to London

"Come on," my good friend, Myra, was coaxing me to travel to London with her. "We'll have a blast," She said. "It's time to come out of your shell and see the world."

"But I can see the entire world on television as well as on my iPad," I snapped back. "I'm not quite ready to travel without Ed. He did all the organizing, planned the trips, and even decided where we should go as well as what we should see. He was my navigator—I was a mere travel companion, I was his sidekick.'

"But your world has changed," Myra said. "Do you really want to just sit home in front of the television and vegetate? Life is for the living, and we have a whole lot of living still to do—especially while we are healthy and strong enough to do so."

Myra had a point. So I agreed and told her to make whatever plans she wanted (within my budget), and that I would be happy to tag along.

Within days, she confessed she had booked us on a two-week theater trip to London, organized by Road Scholar. We would spend a week aboard the Queen Mary 2, where we would enjoy all the amenities of the Cunard ship, plus a whole load of classes and workshops about

London Theater—everything from Shakespearean plays to modern-day musicals. And in London, we would see shows nightly—most of them ones we would have learned about aboard the elegant ship during our trans-Atlantic trip.

The plans were made. The price was paid. As each day passed, I grew more excited, but also a bit more apprehensive. I shopped. I packed. I got my suitcases out of the attic, and hoped—now that everything was up to me—I was doing all the right things. I found my passport, which was hidden somewhere in one of Ed's drawers. It had expired, so I sent away for a new one, which—when it came—I put it in the same drawer with the old one. (Should I keep them both? Since there were no instructions to discard my old one, I kept it.)

The day came to board the ship at the Brooklyn terminal. I lined up for the customs agent to check my passport. "This one is expired," he said. "You can't use it." "What are you talking about?" I shouted, my heart beating so loudly I was sure I would have a heart attack right on the spot.

Sweat poured down my face. I looked around the terminal, and saw hundreds of people going through the gates to the ship. How come I didn't know what they all seemed to know?

Fast forward. Myra boarded the ship and I stayed behind, feeling like the stupidest person on the planet.

A friend invited me to stay at his home in New York, and the following day my sister, who lives near me in Florida, mailed me my current—valid—passport. The following week, I flew to London and met Myra for the last week of the Road Scholar Theater trip. I told myself that half an adventure was better than no trip at all.

But the lesson I learned—reluctantly—was how not to

be reliant on anyone else but myself. What Ed had done for me all of my married life, I now had to do—conscientiously—by myself. This new role is not an easy one, but if I don't figure this all out, I will have to sit home and watch the world go by on my television and my trusty iPad.

My New Friend

Just listen to any love song, and you know instantly that the world travels two by two. Remember "Tea for Two"? Tommy Dorsey's band made that song famous. "Two Silhouettes" (Del Shannon) or "What's Easy for Two is Hard for One," or best yet, "Just the Two of Us..." The world is (and has probably always been) a two-step deal.

But in the world of South Florida Senior Citizens, it's uber-tough to find the other half of a heartthrob, especially for widows. It's a lot easier for widowers, because there are five widows for every man. It's slim pickings for the ladies, but a candy store of goodies for the guys. So until Mr. Perfect—that means any guy who is still able to drive at night—comes along, many of us widowed ladies need to rely on our friends for companionship. And basically, there are two choices:

Choice number one is to continue to go to dinner—or a movie, or whatever activity we select for our evening entertainment—with friends who are still couples. This is sometimes referred to as "The Third-Wheel Syndrome."

That works in the early stage of widowhood when married friends are still kind, solicitous, and often call you to join them for dinner, and even insist that they pay your way. This caring scenario however, is short-lived, and only lasts for a month or two after your spouse passes away.

There are two possible reasons for this—or at least this is what many of my widowed friends have speculated. One is that the *wife* might be irrationally jealous of newly-single lady—especially if she thinks the *NSL* is prettier than she is. Another reason is that the *husband* may want to feel like a hero and "rescue" the grieving damsel in distress. Consequently, the wife—who is usually the social director for the couple—will find endless excuses to exclude the singleton from the couple's future social plans.

Choice number two: is to spend an evening with fellow widowed ladies (ones you might not have been friends with—or might not have even known—before you came to this new stage in your life, but with whom you now share a common bond). Welcome to your new sorority of singles—rah, rah, sis boom bah.

OK. But what about that process of bonding with fellow widowed friends? A girl's night out? An evening to go to a play, a movie or just have dinner together. In the beginning, I accepted invitations from experienced widows who welcomed me into their sorority. I tried going out to dinner with a group of them—maybe six or seven. But as I looked around the restaurant or movie theater (and saw the two-by-two world whizz by), it just didn't seem right to me. Spending an evening with a group of once-grieving gals left me feeling even lonelier than before.

Don't get me wrong—I adore my woman friends. And I genuinely enjoy my daytime activities with them. But when the nighttime comes, I like to be on the arm of a man. But that's just me, and it's a feeling that certainly doesn't apply to everyone.

So what was my third choice? I gave that a lot of thought. My conclusion was to keep working at being both my own best friend, and comfortable in my own skin. It took me time (and many nights alone), but eventually I discovered a whole new world of special interests to keep me company at night.

Thanks to my iPad—which is filled with movies and wonderful books to read—"lonely nights" have disappeared from both my life and my vocabulary. I am now comfortable spending time with myself—whether I have plans with friends for the evening or not. And thanks to Mother Technology, I have a new friend who is available anytime I want.

Taking Out the Garbage

I was married to Ed for 50 years, and never once was I asked to take out the garbage. After all, everyone knows that it's man's job. So it's no wonder that it took me time to get into the routine of filling the heavy-duty black garbage bags, tying them up with those little thingamajigs, tossing them into the large garbage pails, and then schlepping them out to the curb. And it was also a challenge to remember which days the garbage pails got picked up, and which days the recyclables—in their blue and yellow color-coded bins—were collected.

One thing I do know for sure, however, is that this is definitely not a job for a woman who has lovely manicured nails that she carefully polishes on a weekly basis. But in the grand scheme of my new life, hauling the garbage out to the curb is probably one of the easiest new responsibilities of my widowhood. (I said easiest, not nicest!)

As with everything else, it's taken me time to get it right, but not without using every foul-mouthed curse word I've ever learned. I'm not proud to admit that these words—which I would have washed my children's mouths out with soap if they had said them—have now become an intrinsic part of my vocabulary. Especially when I have to do something (even remotely unpleasant) that I've never done before.

But I guess part of moving on is learning how to deal with all the things that I never—in a million years—thought I should, could, or would ever need (or have) to do.

P.S. To help myself be more organized, I tacked a big sign on the garage wall to remind me that the days for garbage pick-up are Wednesdays and Saturdays; recyclables are only collected on Saturdays. I made the sign large enough so that I can read it without putting on my glasses. There is only one glitch in this smart plan of mine—I still need to remember to read the sign.

My Dinner Date with Wolf Blitzer

He might not be particularly good-looking, and perhaps he asks too many questions, but—in a pinch—Wolf Blitzer is a decent dinner companion. You see, when you live alone, chances are that most nights you will dine solo. But I've learned that with Wolf in your kitchen, you won't feel so isolated. And if you listen to the nightly news, you will always have a lot to talk about when you do go out to dinner with friends.

Many nights—especially in the early months of widowhood—I wasn't sure how to navigate dinner dates. Some of my married friends did call and ask me to join them; other friendships went by the wayside. Here in South Florida, the protocol is for friends to pay the widow's dinner the first time they go out—but after that the widow is expected to pay for herself. To avoid any confusion—one friend advised—ask for a separate bill as soon as you are seated.

Another rule of thumb is to first ask where your friends plan to dine. That way you can make sure the cost of the eatery is within your budget, and determine if the restaurant of their choosing serves the kind of food you like to eat.

But sometimes I am so lonely that I will accept an invitation to go anywhere just so I won't have to eat alone. One night—not too long ago—I dined with friends who chose a restaurant that offered a three-course early-bird special. I thought I could resist eating the whole meal because I knew how fattening it was, but I was so happy to socialize over dinner that I didn't realize I'd eaten every last morsel.

But then again, even having dinner all by your lonesome also has the ability to pack on the pounds. Let me explain, these days my meals are, well, whatever I can get my hands on with little—or no—effort. For example, a "meal" might mean a cup of coffee and a good-sized slab of coffee cake.

The other night, however, I did manage to prepare an at-home balanced dinner. For a healthy dose of calcium, I enjoyed a large scoop of ice cream. For the complex carbohydrate portion of my meal, I devoured a half-bag of Stacy's *whole wheat* pita chips. And—for protein—I munched on a fistful of almonds!

Getting back to my televised mealtime companion— let me make it clear that Wolf is not my only dinner date. At my age, I enjoy playing the field. Some nights I like to have dinner with friends—like Mike and Molly or Jerry Seinfeld and his buddies.

When switching channels I found new and interesting people to serve as my dinner companions. I now know that when it comes to my meals—I am simply not ready to go steady.

Money and Rip Van Winkle

Of all the new chores I had to learn to handle after Ed's death—paying the bills and understanding financial investments were the most difficult items on the list.

Silly as it sounds, I compare myself to Rip Van Winkle—the man who ran off into the woods with a flask of his favorite booze, got smashed, and slept under a tree for 20 years! The only difference between good ol' Rip and me is that when it comes to money issues—I was asleep for half a century!!!!

But like Rip, when I awoke, I realized that my world had changed big time. Washington Irving—the celebrated author of this famed fable—pointed out that change is inevitable. And he added, you pay a huge price by trying to avoid all those things that refuse to stay the same. And looking back to those early months of widowhood—the cost of my denial hit real hard.

For many years before Ed died, he would often suggest that I go over the bills with him, and sit in on the investment advisor's meetings, and understand how to negotiate our tax consequences with the IRS. But—try as he might—I had "more important things" to take care of—like my weekly manicure or monthly hair cut. Plus,

I'd much rather go on a shopping spree with my girlfriends or have lunch at some special café than reconcile our checkbook, or file our income tax returns.

After Ed died, as the bills began to pile up, I merely tossed them into a large plastic garbage bag. Then I placed the bag into a closet, where it would be totally out of sight. *I'll take care of the payments, one of these days*, I fantasized. But, truth be told, I was hoping that a fairy godmother would fly into my house, and save me from this job that I never—not in a million years—thought I would have to tackle. And let me tell you—for a grown woman who still has to count on her fingers—it was too scary to face tackling this most important chore.

Although I was in total denial, there were several days—during those early months—when I had a frequent and frightening nightmare that I'd become a bag lady.

After weeks—maybe it was even months—of feeling frozen, I began to behave like a grown-up and slowly started to take note of who gets paid what and how much. Oh yes, I made a few mistakes—actually a lot more than a few. Shock waves would go through me every time I received a note from a company with big red letters that said, "OVERDUE" or the interest charges I needed to shell out because I hadn't paid my credit card bill on time.

I must say—as of this writing—which is slightly more than two years into widowhood that (a) I finally can now pay my bills on time, (b) I've become quite adept at keeping to budget (better than Ed ever did), and (c) actually understand what's being said when my broker talks about municipal bonds, ETF's REITs and whether preferred stocks are really, well, preferred.

And more than anything else, I've learned to call upon good friends in the know—like (a) my friend, Pat, who has a PhD in accounting, (b) my neighbor, Phyllis (who worked as the head teller in a bank prior to her retirement) and (c) Suzy Orman, whose finance book I now read as if it were like a Bible.

So, I guess the moral of this essay is that although I had been monetarily asleep for way too many years when it came to my finances, by the time I finally awoke, I was able to hit the ground running.

What the Hell Do I Want?

It was an evening filled with laughter and the warm camaraderie of good friends; with—of—course plenty of merlot, all of which made our time together **uber** festive.

As we gossiped about the important stuff in our lives—like the best plastic surgeon in town, the 100% fail proof weight-loss plan, and the short list of locally available eligible men who don't need walkers to get around (or the few ones who can still drive at night) I felt that—at last—I could still have plenty of fun, even as a single senior.

My friends dropped me off, and waved goodbye. But when I put the key in the lock and opened the front door—my home's darkness and silence hit me hard. The loneliness factor kicked in full tilt. I'd never imagined that silence could be so deafening, or that stillness could make me feel like I was the only lonely person on the planet. The realization—once again—that *I am all alone* was still as painful as an unexpected bee sting, and as hurtful as being hit on the head by the sharp corner of an overhead cabinet door that has been left ajar.

It was during those excruciating "home alone moments" that I began to ponder the possibilities of sharing my life (and my too-silent home) with someone else.

But with whom would I want to do that? Am I ready to be a significant other? Do I know a man who would fit the double bill of a lover and a companion? Right now, the answer is a deafening "No."

But before I could even think about scouting for someone to fit into my future, I know that I needed to make a few adjustments. I had to find a way to ease those lonesome blues. So here's what I did:

1. For starters, before I would go out for the evening, I would turn all the living room lights on so I'd walk into brightness after unlocking the front door. And I'd keep the radio and television blaring to overpower the echoing silence that pains me so.

2. Then, when I became more comfortable coming into my house alone, I realized that the more I lived (and cared) for myself, the more confident I felt regarding the fact that living alone is really not so bad. In fact, there were some surprisingly comfortable benefits to being a single lady.

3. As a wife, it had always been my job to dust and sweep and keep our home neat and tidy. For decades I would routinely put freshly laundered and folded underwear in Ed's drawer. As a wife, I was in charge of the daily "What's for dinner?" dilemma. So—for half a century—I did the shopping, the cooking, plus the cleaning up afterwards. And I did it day in and day out. Now it's just me for dinner—and a couple of scrambled eggs is good enough. Shopping, cooking and cleaning up afterwards is something

of the long-ago past. And even better—living alone has given me the pleasure of munching on a peanut butter and jelly sandwich while nested in bed at 3 am with no one to ask, "Do you really need to eat that here?"

4. And another perk of living alone is being able to buy fewer rolls of toilet paper, and changing the bed linens only when I'm in the mood.

But is living "easy" an adequate compensation for living "solo"? Maybe, maybe not. Even while I was married, there were many days and nights when loneliness sneaked in unannounced. The marriage certificate may have hung over us as we slept, its loving message was often absent from our bed.

Our ugly arguments or fights over money and in-law issues would send each of us to different corners of the marital ring. Sometimes we could come to an agreement, and move on with our love. But there were many times when the anger would fester, and leave no space for either loving solace or affection.

Is the feeling of loneliness *when you are not alone* measurably different from what you feel when you are? For me, frankly, it's the simply slightly different versions of same pain.

So I guess the lesson I learned from my wrestling match with loneliness is to (a) allow myself to fully feel the pain, the loss and the emptiness, (b) convince myself that it will pass, and then (c) open the shutters to let those aching emotions escape out and away into thin air.

BEA LEWIS

Cleaning Out the Closets

Is it crazy that I didn't want to clear out Ed's closet? After all, wouldn't any woman want an extra closet, so she wouldn't have to stuff all her clothes and shoes into just one small space?

It took me about six months before I could even think about it. As long as I could see Ed's jackets and slacks lined up so neatly—hanger by hanger—in his closet, I felt tangibly connected to him.

But then, a caring friend told me that there were many men in our part of the world who would benefit from having some of his sweaters, his dress slacks and sports jackets. "It's sort of selfish," she said, "to hang onto his belongings—especially those lovely, colorful Tommy Bahama shirts he so loved to wear."

My friend was right, but I wasn't ready to empty out his closet. Because if I did, I would have to face the harsh reality that Ed was gone—forever. And, frankly, I didn't think I could ever pass his empty closet without feeling terribly sad and missing him all over again.

Some of my friends who are fellow widows, cleared their husband's closets within days of the funeral. And I know others who asked their relatives to do the job for them.

Still others—actually one other good friend—confided that she felt safe whenever she sat on the floor of her husband's closet, and smelled his clothes. At the time, I thought that her strange ritual sounded a bit weird. But who am I to judge anyone else's personal timetable for getting past the oh-so-grim grieving stage.

Deciding when to do this difficult job is akin to standing on the edge of a diving board, but not quite being ready to jump into the pool. It's that heart-pounding, fearful feeling that you know you have to do it, but what you really want is to turn around, go down the ladder, and get your two feet safely back on the ground.

What motivated me to finally tackle this painful chore was the fact that far-away friends were coming to visit me and I needed to make room for their belongings. This was my long-overdue incentive to at least get started, and begin to (a) take the slacks and shirts off the hangers, and then (b) move the sweaters and sweatshirts out of his drawers.

But what if I were to give one of his favorite sweaters away, and then later regret that I should have held onto it for a little bit longer? How could I so freely toss out his navy-blue cashmere double-breasted jacket he so proudly wore at our grandson's bar mitzvah?

I must say, however, that there were a few items I was glad to toss out. For example, that too-tight-fitting black shirt, which I absolutely detested. I used to think that he wore it just to annoy me. (Oh, how I'd love to have that "annoyance" back again!) I was also glad to get rid of those flashy ties he loved to wear, and—oh yes—the frayed jeans that were so baggy in the rear.

Grief counselors tell us that the process of clearing out can be agonizing because each little item we toss triggers memories of when and where it was worn. But several friends—who had been there before me—offered some suggestions that helped me cope with this most stressful experience. For example, they advised me—before I begin to sort and toss—to get several boxes, permanent markers and garbage bags for all the inconsequential junk that accumulated over the years.

There will, of course, be some things that you will never want to part with. For example, I will always cherish the letters and cards we gave each other over the years. Ed had saved them in a box he kept on a shelf in his closet. (From time to time, I would take these out of the container, read our inscriptions, and—with a bunch of tissues—have myself a good cry.)

Ed's closet might be empty now, but my heart will be always filled with the wonderful memories of the things we did together, what we meant to each other, as well as all of the clothes—beautiful and otherwise—that he used to wear.

You Can't Go Back Again

Recently as I was glancing at a group of old photographs, I came to an abrupt stop when I saw a picture of Ed and me that had been snapped at a friend's daughter's wedding. I was dressed in a black chiffon dress, and Ed was decked out in a designer tuxedo with a colorful bow tie.

The picture had been taken decades ago—we both were in our forties, preoccupied with paying the monthly mortgage payment and other bills, while busy raising our three daughters. It was a hectic time, during which we had been taking care of everything and everyone except ourselves.

As I looked at the picture, I could see that Ed's jacket was open because it had been too tight around his belly to be buttoned. I remember how annoyed I 'd been back then that he refused to close his jacket—no matter how many times I pestered him to do so. Did that "disagreement" put a damper on the evening? To be totally honest, it did. I nagged at him, and he got annoyed. And just like a recalcitrant young teenager who does the opposite of whatever you want him or her to do—Ed would willfully let his jacket flap in the wind, not caring a bit how unkempt I thought he looked.

In hindsight, when I recall that night—and numerous other times when the most insignificant things got my goat—I realized how foolishly I had behaved. Was I annoyed that he didn't look "perfectly groomed" or "well dressed" in my eyes? Was I worried that the world at large would judge him? Or would they—much more disconcerting—judge me for not adequately overseeing his wardrobe choices? Today, I so regret that I allowed such a silly sartorial non-issue to put a damper on what should have been a totally joyful evening.

Another equally annoying incident happened one day when I came home late from work—tired, cranky and hungry—only to find the kitchen sink piled high with dirty dishes, and the dinner I had planned for myself, totally ransacked. "You are so inconsiderate," I yelled at Ed, without remembering—at that time—that his priority was helping the girls with their math, because the next day our daughters were scheduled to take an achievement test at school.

Was I angry at Ed for being "inconsiderate"? Maybe, but I now realize that I had really been annoyed at myself for not being the ideal, flawless, thoughtful Mom. You know, the kind of Mom who would have come home from work early in order to help her daughters prepare for their important exam.

I remember how often I bitched whenever Ed would leave his dirty clothes on the floor (we did have a hamper, but he rarely used it), or when he would "forget" to put a new supply of toilet paper in the bathroom after he'd used the last sheets on a roll. How easy it is—with my now perfect 20/20 hindsight—to wallow in the sludge of the past, which lies in the dark, deep recesses of our soul.

Sadly, nothing that we've done in the past can ever be changed.

But now that Ed is gone, I actually ache for those petty annoyances, and long to have **do-over** with him. But—as so many people have noted—life is not a dress rehearsal. These days, I need to learn how to move forward and adjust to being "just me." This is hard work, especially when the loneliness hits me squarely in the gut.

But hey, I'm no stranger to challenges. I once ran in a 5K race. And even though I was the last to cross the finish line, I still managed to complete the course. Today, it often seems like my "new" life will resemble training for a challenging marathon—widowhood veterans have told me that I need to be ready for the possibility of one day (perhaps) finding love again. And if I do, I've promised myself to never be upset if I come home to a sink full of dirty dishes.

Why? The answer is obvious. That's why G-d created restaurants.

What's My Label?

When you are married, they call you *Mrs.*

When you are single, it's *Ms.*

When you get an engagement ring, you're known as somebody's *fiancée.*

If you are in a gay relationship, you are someone's *partner.*

If you're going with a college frat boy—they say you are *pinned.*

If you are dating different guys, they say you are *playing the field.*

If you are only dating one man—you are *going steady.*

But in the senior dating world, the labels can be quite different. Take me, for example. At this point in time, I am 77 years-old and I am dating a man who is 91. If I refer to him as my *boyfriend,* I think my grandchildren would howl with laughter. But if I refer to him as my *gentleman friend,* I would feel like a stodgy old lady.

My friend Lew, too, says he feels young when he refers to me as his *girlfriend*, although he often wonders if it isn't politically correct—at this age—to say he has a *lady friend.*

Not long ago, a friend said she had a lovely man she wanted me to meet. "I'm sorry," I said, "but I'm *seeing someone.*" My friend—who is my contemporary—knew exactly what I meant. But if I had said that to a person decades younger, they might have wondered if I had a vision problem.

One step beyond dating is *living together*. In days gone by, such a couple would be considered *living in sin*. But in the senior dating world, this is a perfectly acceptable way of life. For no other reason than when two people share the household expenses, there is more money to spend to go on cruises.

And what if you are living together only on weekends? I have a neighbor who lives part time with her (as she refers to him) *significant other* because, she explained, she can go to her own house whenever he gets on her nerves!"

Before I met Lew, I had dated a few other men. I labeled one man *Cheap Bob* because he considered going to Wendy's as a perfectly acceptable dinner date. I called another one *Deaf Man* because he never heard a word I said. Looking back, I wonder if he really couldn't hear me or if he was so used to tuning out whatever his wife had talked about that not responding to *anything* I said was just a habit! And the most accurate label I ever gave to a man was reserved for a gentleman who thought he could drive at night. Unfortunately, his vision was so impaired that he was really a danger on the road. My name for him became *Near Death* and, frankly, we only dated once—for obvious reasons. In retrospect, as far as I'm concerned, he was a "blind date" in more ways than one…

The other day I was having lunch with some lady friends, one of whom had just lost her *significant other*—or the man she had lived with for twelve years.

Before Joe passed away, she told me, she had been married to Frank for 47 years. When Frank had died, she became a *widow*, but what do we call her now that the man she lived with for more than a decade has died, as well? I think a new label is in order. I can't think of one, except to say, "Gee, I am so very, very sorry for your loss."

BEA LEWIS

Am I Sliding Back?

It was a happy time for my family. My first-born grandchild was getting married. As I packed my bag—with the new black chiffon dress I had purchased for the occasion—I felt so sad. What was going on? I should have been ecstatic. But, instead I was an unsmiling glum chum.

As I traveled to the airport to fly from Florida to Baltimore, I was really glad that I hadn't brushed on mascara because tears filled up in my eyes and rolled down my cheeks. Was I sad because it seemed like only yesterday that Lyn was just a little baby girl whom I held in my arms and rocked to sleep? Was it because she was gay and getting married to a woman? No, I thought. *These are not reasons to cry. My granddaughter is ecstatic. And happily, in the year 2015, this beloved child is free to live her authentic self.*

So what's this all about, I asked myself. *What are these tears for?* Then, out of the blue, I had a realization—something like what Oprah describes as an *Aha! moment*, the time when you suddenly understand a painful truth. Duh!

Those tears were for the past life that Ed and I shared—the home we built, the children we raised—and the dreams we had to see our family grow and prosper. So that's it. *Again, it's all about wanting you to be with me, Ed. Damn, when will I stop missing you?*

But, Ed, I say to myself, *for these special occasions regarding our children or grandchildren (or even if I live long enough to have some great-grandchildren) I have to find a way to share these glorious moments with you—even if it's just in my thoughts. Wherever you are—I hope you can hear me.*

MOVING ON

You cannot prevent the birds of sorrow from flying over your head, but you can stop them from nesting in your hair.

Eva Ibbotson

Senior Dating 101

A friend of 60 years called to ask me to dinner. He and I—and his late wife—had been high school classmates. When my husband of half a century passed away, my two friends came to Ed's funeral. A year later, I paid my respects when his wife lost her six-year cancer battle.

Knowing that I'd been widowed sometime before him, my old classmate called to talk. "I think I'm ready to date, but I don't have the foggiest notion of where or how to begin. Maybe you could offer some suggestions."

As we dined together at Flakowitz (a popular local deli), we shared stories of the comings and goings of our high school classmates—who had died, who was living in Florida, and which ones we still saw socially.

It was a crowded night, and our table for two was close to another small one where a couple—about our age—was seated.

Being somewhat of a *yenta*, I noticed that neither the man nor his lady companion was wearing wedding bands. I leaned over to my friend and whispered, "I think that couple is on a date." Curious about how the "daters" were negotiating the single life, my companion turned up

81

his hearing aid.

As we listened, we learned that, just like us, both were widowed. And just like us, both were trying to figure out how to get on with their lives after losing a spouse with whom they'd spent decades together.

As we eavesdropped, we overheard the lady offer to pay for her meal. "Don't be silly. This is Flakowitz, not the Four Seasons." Her gentleman friend responded.

But what if this were the Four Seasons, my friend and I wondered? Would a gentleman then accept her offer to share the bill? And if a lady asks a man for a dinner date, does she pay, or does a true gentleman insist that the dinner is on him?

We then discussed another dating dilemma. When we were young, no self-respecting girl would accept a last-minute invitation. A guy had to call a girl no later than Wednesday for a Saturday night date. The rationale, if I remember it correctly, was that if she were to accept a last-minute date, it meant that she had had no other offers. Her ego—and her popularity status—was seriously at stake.

In the senior dating world, however, the rule is "no standing on ceremony." A 15-minute advance call is just fine. (Although a lady of a certain age does need a few minutes to put on some lipstick and check out her skinniest – looking jeans before going out on a date.)

Another new rule revolves around the issue of driving. In our young dating days, the guy would ALWAYS pick up his date. But in our senior world it's perfectly acceptable for the lady to be behind the wheel, especially if the gentleman can no longer drive safely at night.

Our evening ended, and I remembered the old-fashioned, proper girl of my youth never allowed kissing on a first date. But now??? PULEEZE. Life is way too short to miss out on any opportunity for even a single moment of pleasure. (And my dinner companion heartily agreed!)

Beware of a Fix up

A friend in New York telephoned to say that she had a single friend who'd just moved to Boca Raton. She thought we should meet each other, so I agreed and said, "Have him call me."

Before I tell you the rest of the story, Dear Reader, I must be honest and reveal that I am a woman who has always been self-conscious about my weight. And even though I'm an "ordinary" size, I've rarely been a successful dieter.

I am a recidivistic Weight Watcher drop-out (at least 40 times over the years), and I'm probably the only idiot who (a) got suckered into believing the TV ads for the Quick Weight Loss Diet, (b) gained five pounds when I went on their "guaranteed" plan, and (c) wound up $200 poorer. Not to mention that—back in the days when I went on the Cabbage Soup diet—I wound up in the emergency room with what I was sure was a heart attack. I'm embarrassed to admit that it was only a severe case of gastric issues. I could bore you with a lengthy list of all my other attempts at weight loss, but I think you get the picture.

So, let's get back to my fix-up tale. The Boca singleton called me, and after we'd spent a few minutes on the usual banter ("When did you move here?" "When did you lose your husband?" "Where do the kids live?" etc. etc.), I began to relax. Then out of left field, he asked me a question that no weight-conscious, size-sensitive female would ever want to hear.

"Bea, what size dress do you wear?' he asked. I wasn't sure that I'd heard right, but he then quickly repeated, "What is your dress size?" I was, to say the least, taken aback by his unusual question, and—literally—speechless.

But then, giving him the benefit of the doubt, I thought that perhaps he was a dress manufacturer who wanted to give me—as a gift—a few samples from his potentially impressive line.

Wary of letting anyone—especially a stranger of the opposite sex—know either my dress size or how much I weigh, I decided to make sure his curiosity was based on kindness. So I asked him why he wanted to know. "Well," he answered, "to tell the truth, I only like slender women."

Not sure of his definition of the word "slender," I asked, "What does *slender* mean to you?" "Oh", he answered, "I like it if a woman is a size four, but a size six would do."

Now here's where you need to know yet another truth about me. I am one of those women who is ecstatic when I can comfortably squeeze into a size 12! But I digress. Not wanting to insult my well-meaning girlfriend who'd suggested we "get to know each other," I agreed to meet Mr. Skinny-Seeker for lunch at Too-Jay's the following day. (He probably had a coupon.)

But when I got off the phone, I thought "There is no way I would ever want to meet—much less spend time with—such a narrow-minded, narcissistic male version of a Boca Babe." So I made an escape plan, and called him the following morning to say that when I'd woken up I'd had a sore throat. I, therefore, would sadly not be able to make our meeting. (I weakly coughed into the phone a few times for audio authenticity.)

I then called my long-distant matchmaker friend in New York, and told her the truth. And that's when she said, "You know, I haven't seen or spoken to him for about 15 years, and—actually—he did seem a little crazy back then. I guess that with age, he became even crazier."

So the moral of this tale is to beware of any social fix-ups, especially ones from well-meaning, long-term far-away girlfriends.

The Brisket Brigade

I must confess, I never cared much for brisket, the fatty part of the cow that—for centuries—Jewish home cooks have embraced for holiday dinners and celebration.

While I knew—well before I became a widow that to win the heart of a potential mate, significant other or lover I would need to be a brisket-making maven. *But,* I wondered, *where did this written-in-stone tradition come from?* Especially since, (these days, at least) we are well aware that eating too much artery-clogging cholesterol should be off limits for any potential partner beyond a certain age.

According to legend, the tradition comes from the Eastern European *shtetls*. When a widow learned that a man in her town had lost his wife, she'd swiftly go to her stove to cook up a pot of care and concern. You could compare this activity to a fisherman who tosses his line into the waters with hopes that he will reel in a big fluke or tuna. The difference, however, between the hopeful fisherman and the lonely widow who cooks a brisket is that the fisherman can afford to be patient. But unlike the fisherman—who must sit and wait—speed is of the essence if the widow wants to beat out her competition. Even back during the *shtetl* days, the ratio of widowed women to men was out of balance. Today it's even worse. In fact, a recent US census reported that of the 13 million widowed folk over the age of 65—11 million are women.

But, why a brisket? Well, back in the olden days, when meat was scarce and expensive, bringing a brisket to the grieving widower showed that—when it came to how she felt about his wellbeing—no expense should be spared.

While I now understand where this brisket tradition came from, I still needed to know why the custom is often referred to as the "Brisket Brigade." I think I finally found the answer. One day, as I sunbathed in my backyard, a swarm of ants came crawling to feast on the crumbs I'd dropped on the patio from my oversized Dunkin' Donut muffin. They marched swiftly—as if in lockstep formation—and I knew exactly what they were doing. They were organized and determined, almost like well-drilled soldiers out for the kill.

These little guys knew (much like all modern-day savvy widows) that the first in line had the best chance of beating out the others.

But these days, just bringing a widower a cooked brisket might not be enough to fight the fierce competition. Nowadays you need an edge. A friend of mine, who is a widower, told me recently that along with the directions about how to reheat his meal in a microwave, one widow had added her phone number along with a flattering photo of herself that had (obviously) been taken decades earlier.

Since I don't like making brisket—never made it and never will—I guess I must find another way to entice an appealing man with my culinary skills. I could bake a fresh batch of my marvelous nut-studded Jewish cookies called mandelbread (but for the single men with dentures, I would leave out the nuts).

But if neither my cooking nor baking skills fit the bill, I guess I will just have to depend on my good looks, warmth, charm, wit and charismatic and fun-loving (and, of course, humble) personality to win the heart of a very special man.

Going on a First Date

About three months after Ed passed away, a widower—who was a friend of a friend—called to see how I was doing.

"Not great," I answered. "I know what you are going through," he said. "It's tough. But let me cheer you up and take you to dinner."

At first, I hesitated to go. But, it was past the 30-day mourning period (called the *shloshem*), and—according to Jewish law—it would be OK to gradually reenter everyday life.

But more than abiding by Jewish law, I worried what my friends and neighbors would think about me if they saw me having dinner with a single man.

After some soul searching, I agreed to accept his invitation because I figured a widower had probably already gone through his own loss, and would be able to understand what I was feeling. And to boot, I was so lonely—eating in front of the TV each night watching financial news on MSNBC and trying to understand this new language—that if a monkey had asked me to dinner, I would have probably welcomed the opportunity to share a meal.

The evening began rather sweetly, as we each shared our stories of losing a spouse. But then my date went on to tell me how HE was coping, how HE was learning to cook and care for HIS beautiful home. I also heard about the new car HE had bought to cheer HIMSELF up, and the many (make that VERY many) women who were contacting HIM on JDate.com, the internet dating site for Jewish singles.

The conversation was more like a monologue (HIS), rather than a dialogue between two people who were trying to figure out how to intelligently get on with their lives.

Our dinner reservations were at a local fish restaurant, and—for a man who had mentioned that financially he was "way more than just comfortable" he paid with a coupon that offered the holder two dinners for the price of one! Perhaps—I thought to myself—that was the key to his affluence.

As I drizzled dressing onto my salad, and buttered my hot seeded roll, my widower friend noticed that my hands were shaking. "Relax," he whispered. "The first time you do anything at this stage of our lives, it will feel somewhat uncomfortable."

I wondered what he meant about "the first time you do something." Was he hinting about something more intimate than I could possibly even think about? Just the idea of such a thing made me so nervous that I guzzled down my glass of wine!

With each bite of the halibut that I'd ordered, my mind drifted back to his comment. How could a nice Jewish girl from the Bronx—and the only one in my crowd who'd remained a virgin until she married—even entertain such a thought. ("Oh, yes, waiter, I would

LOVE another glass of wine, please!")

As I gobbled up my roasted potatoes, I realized that I felt sad. Hadn't my widower friend of a friend offered to cheer ME up? Wasn't HE supposed to lend ME a shoulder to cry on? But as HE continued to talk about HIS enviable life, it was hard to concentrate. Why? Because I couldn't help but notice the pieces of spinach that were stuck between HIS teeth.

The evening had begun with a sense of expectation and anticipation, but by the time it was over, all I could feel was disappointment, and an even more intense level of loneliness.

Back at home later that night, I couldn't help but wonder if this dating thing would ever feel "right" to me. But as the old expression goes, (and as I mentioned in the introduction) I guess you need to—especially after a good 50-year marriage—kiss a lot of frogs before you find your Prince.

So, for me, it's one unkissed frog down. Next…

Looking For Love on the Internet

We met on JDate. My profile listed that I like long strolls along the beach, hiking at local state parks. He read my profile, gave me a wink, and wrote that he liked to do the same types of things. Wow! I felt like I had won the jackpot. We agreed to get together for coffee the following night. When we met at Dunkin' Donuts (he had a coupon), we realized that we had more in common than just walking and hiking. We had both been married for a half-century, and we had both been caregivers to our seriously ill spouses.

A year older than I—he was tall and slender, except for a slightly protruding belly—Joe was in good health and, like me, anxious to move on with his life. He was also searching for new interests, and trying to understand what he wanted to experience during his remaining years—or at least for the next few months. Me, too!

Joe and I dated often, and together we enjoyed movies, dinners, mile-long walks, and the occasional theater production. He took me out for a St. Valentine dinner (it was an early bird special) and he bought me a Valentine card (which he'd found at the dollar store)!

When we weren't together, Joe would call to remind me to go to my Pilates class, and he truly seemed concerned and caring. I met his friends and children, and he met mine.

(What's interesting is that my daughter didn't care for him, nor did any of my friends. "He's boring," said one. "He needs to cut the hairs out of his nose," said another. And the biggest bugaboo (or should I say clue) was when we went to have dinner with friends and he didn't want to share "his coupon" with the other couple!!!!)

Sometimes we'd just hang out at each other's houses. We would frequently bring in dinner, and then watch his favorite television show, *Shark Tank*, together. Those hours were both relaxing and comforting. With that kind of consistent friendship, it never entered my mind that Joe might be simultaneously seeing another woman. I certainly was not interested in dating anyone else.

But then—like a surprise attack or an exploding grenade—everything changed. I remember the exact moment when Joe hit me with the news that there was another woman in his life.

After a delightful morning walk on the beach, I had asked Joe if he'd like to come over that evening to watch an episode of *Homeland*. It was a TV show that we had often discussed and we would try to second guess which characters were the good guys—and which were the bad ones. "No," he answered a bit sheepishly. "I have a dinner date." He followed that unexpected news bulletin with "I've been meaning to tell you that I have been seeing another lady. I actually met her before I met you, and I like you both."

After letting his words sink in, sharply inhaling and silently counting to ten, I asked, "how's that possible, Joe, when we are together so many days each week?" "Well," he said, "I only see her now and then. I am just not ready to make a commitment to seeing only you."

"Joe, what are you talking about? I never asked you for a commitment," I said, "I've been enjoying what we had, and just wanted to let nature take its course. But now, Joe, I am so dumbfounded by what you just said that I think it's best if you leave."

Like a naughty school boy whose mother had caught him in a lie, he turned around and walked to the door. His eyes were twitching, a habit that I'd noticed only happened when he was nervous. It was a good thing that he left before my rage got the best of me. I'd been tempted to throw a coffee pot at him. Instead I reached for my best friend, who lies in the freezer, my oversized bottle of vodka. I drank, and then I slept, which is my usual (preferred) way to deal with whatever emotional pain comes my way.

Throughout the night—through the tears—I gave serious thought to what had just happened to my previously enjoyable relationship. I didn't close my eyes for an instant. By the time the sun rose the next morning, I realized that I had been duped.

How could I have not known? How could I have been deceived by someone who seemed to care for me so genuinely? At least I did learn a valuable lesson about dating, which is to go slow, and not be so trusting. When you're married to one person for half a century, trust is part of the package. But it's not necessarily so when you are just dating.

Joe was gone for good. But it was now time for some "reality check" questions. What was it about me that made me so needy for affection? Did I really "need" a man in my life? Even one who was so deceitful? Why hadn't I been able to see what had been right in front of my face? Or, perhaps the better question was: What allowed me to willfully refuse to see the reality (clearly obvious to everyone else) that was right before my eyes?

Obviously, I had a lot of soul searching to do, and I needed to work hard to understand how and why I could be so naïve or stupid. Right now, what was most important was to do what my friends had been telling me to do all along (but which I couldn't bear to hear at the time). They had wanted me to think better of myself, and to feel worthy that only "the best" would be deserving of my love. Can that ever happen? I hope so. But for now I realize that I need to be totally happy having just me. It's time for Bea to become Bea's best friend.

It's Not So Bad Being Alone

The other night I awoke feeling hungry. I knew there was some cookie dough ice cream in the freezer that I had purchased when there was a two for one sale at Publix.

Who could resist such a bargain? I planned to keep the two for one deal in my freezer because you never know when friends will stop by to visit! But who was I fooling? I know that no one "just stops by" without an invitation or at least an advance phone call.

So I proactively said to myself, "Bea, don't you dare take any." But at 3 am one morning, believe it or not, that ice cream was singing a siren song. "Come to me, love me, I will bring you much joy."

Ok, ok, how much damage could just a few spoonfuls do?

Although I was in the process of breaking promises that I had made to myself, who would know? There was no one around to stop me. No spouse to be disturbed if I were to get out of bed, and go into the kitchen. No husband to ask me, "Do you really need that?"

And the best part was that I could take one of the bargain pints back into my cozy, disheveled bed, and slowly take spoonful after spoonful of the cold, artificially-flavored, chemically-enhanced vanilla-flavored ice cream with large chunks of pasteurized cookie dough until it was—ALL—gone.

Bereavement experts tell widow to "live in the moment." So I told myself that I was just following orders. And to improve the cookie-dough ice cream moment, I turned on the TV to watch reruns of the reality show, *The Real Housewives of New Jersey.*

Total decadence, total guilty pleasure, total happiness! Is there any greater gift a bereaving widow can give herself? What a perfect way to cheer herself up in the loneliness of the dark, dark night. Now tell me, could I have sneaked a high-calorie late night snack like that if I had a spouse snoring alongside me? No way. Of course, if I had a choice, I would have preferred to have my darling Ed lying close to me with one arm clasped lovingly around my waist.

But feeling that cold, sweet goodness slowly go down my esophagus—especially while watching a stupid reality show at 3am—was pretty terrific. I'm willing to concede that it was potentially—perhaps—the second best scenario for me.

Home is Where the Heart Is

My friend, Donna, who lost her husband around the same time that Ed passed away, was busy redecorating her house. With an enthusiastic grin, she told me, "It's my way of moving forward and knowing that I can do whatever pleases me. I don't have to get anyone's approval."

This was a big deal for Donna, whose husband had—for the duration of their 40-year marriage—made all the decisions. After many decades of giving in (rather than fighting), she finally had the chance to do whatever made her happy. And she could do it without needing her husband's—or anyone else's—approval. "I've stopped anticipating what others need. I am now my first priority, and it feels damn good."

And when it came to fixing up her beloved home, boy, did she run with it. I told her, "What you've done is symbolic in some fashion." Then I asked, "But why the house? Couldn't you think of some more interesting ways to validate your independence?"

Donna explained, "Well, my house is a metaphor for who I am in my life right now. Every time I change the wallpaper or paint a wall a different color, there is no one there to tell me what to do, how to do it, when to do it— or even if I should do anything at all.

"It's taken me a long time to feel at home in my own skin. And making this house in my own image has helped me to become a person who is comfortable, peaceful and secure without a husband at her side."

I asked Donna, "But what if you met a potential husband?"

"Frankly," she told me, "my house has become the significant man in my life. And a great man at that," she laughed.

"I'm not sure that I understand," I told her. "Well, let me explain. This house will never leave me. This house never talks back. This house is happy because it looks a whole lot better than before. This house appreciates whatever I do, whether I paint the walls a robin's egg blue or add a moss green couch or toss out the ratty leather chair that I needed to keep because it was for the man of the house. Now it's all about what makes the lady of the house happy—and, boy, does it feel good.

"Best yet," she continued, "when it's just my house, it's only my mess. If my house is neat and orderly when I leave in the morning, you can rest assured that it will still be neat and orderly when I return home at night. My house never questions where I am going or when I will return. It just says, 'See you later, have a good time.'

"And when I return after a busy fun day from shopping and having lunch with the girls, my house never asks me how much money I spent or questions about when dinner will be ready. It just beckons me to kick off my shoes, put on the stereo, grab a glass of Pinot Grigio, and restore myself in quiet solitude."

Recently, Donna treated herself to a set of floral

sheets. "For the first time in 40 years I can slide into my bedroom garden of fabric roses, and feel like a very pampered princess. A man in my life would have said, 'Too feminine.'

For me, it was interesting to hear about a recently widowed woman's take on living alone and moving on. It was a completely different experience—and perspective—than my own. While I moved on and embraced independence differently, I was happy to learn that there's more than one way to celebrate one's self.

And above all, her story made me feel truly grateful that for over five decades it had never been Ed's house or Bea's house. Instead, it had always been **our home**.

The Wrong Number

To keep myself busy—and to be in a place where I could meet new friends—I agreed to volunteer at the monthly singles get-togethers at my local Jewish Community Center. My job as a hostess was to offer coffee and cookies to the participants.

On one of those evenings, an unusually cold February night, a rather nice-looking gentleman asked me for milk to pour into his coffee. I brought it to him, offered him a wooden stirrer, and—when he thanked me—I felt a slight charge of I guess you could call it electricity or perhaps you would call it "attraction" for him.

"Thank you," he said, and then he glanced at my name tag and noticed that my last name—Lewis was the same as his first name. We laughed, and I said, "We could start a law firm—Lewis and Lewis." When he reached over to the serving plate with the confections, he offered me a chocolate chip cookie, which he said were his favorite.

He then made a comment that totally confused me. "You have lovely teeth," he said. WHHHAAT??? I thought he'd said, "You have lovely tits." So I asked him to explain what he had just said. "Your teeth," he repeated, "are in good shape." Oh, I thought he had said something quite different. I was relieved when he explained. "I'm a dentist—I notice those things." PHHEWWW!

When that misunderstanding was cleared up, we began a conversation that lasted a good 20 minutes. In that time, I learned that Lew was also widowed, had been a long-time caregiver for his late-wife, and—as he'd already told me—a retired dentist. He seemed impressed that I was a retired journalist, who had worked for a newspaper that he knew of (but never had read).

Our banter flowed easily. I felt so comfortable talking with him, and he later told me that he'd felt the same way.

"Would you like to go out for dinner some night," he asked, "so we can continue our conversation? I'd like to learn more about you," he said. Then he asked for my telephone number. Believe it or not, I was so nervous and rattled that my hands were shaking. And accidentally, I wrote a 9 instead of a 7.

Days passed, and I was disappointed that I hadn't heard from him. "Oh well," I thought, "he probably asked all the single women at that night's lecture for their phone numbers."

A week later, I got a call from the JCC hospitality coordinator to let me know a gentleman had tried to call me, but seemed to have the wrong telephone number. Obviously, she could not give him my contact information, but asked for his phone number which she would give to me.

I immediately called Lew, who said he was so very happy to hear from me! We made dinner plans, and when he came to pick me up, Lew showed me the wrong number I had given him. He said he was determined to track me down.

As I was getting ready for our first date, I tried on five different outfits. I really wanted to make sure that I looked my best. (I went with the beige slacks paired with a brown sweater, and because I remember that Lew was not much taller than I am, I slipped on a pair of brown suede flats.)

My hands were shaking when he rang the door bell, but when I opened the front door and saw his sweet face and warm smile, I quickly calmed down. In that moment, I was so very happy to see—and to have a diner date with—this terrific guy.

A Stranger in the Night

On the drive home from my first date with Lew, the radio played a Frank Sinatra song—Strangers in the Night. "I love that song," Lew said, and at the next red light, as he stepped on the brake, he placed his right hand on my left knee cap.

It was a moment of decision—"Do I think the man is too brazen and push his hand away—after all this was our very first date—or do I go with the flow of the romantic moment?" (I did the latter!)

Sixteen months later and that song still haunts us both as deeply as during the moment when we first heard it together. That was when we both knew that we would want to see each other again.

Strangers in the Night...
Two lonely people, we were strangers in the night
Up to that moment when we said our first hello,
Little did we know
That Love was just a glance away
A warm embracing dance away

Conventional wisdom teaches us that mature adults should not be starry-eyed—after all, that's a teenager's version of romance. "Take time to get to know the other person," the experts advise, "learn about his or her character traits and goals in life before you even consider entering a relationship."

But with maturity also comes the instinctive and immediate wisdom to know what will—or will not—work.

Strangers in the Night,
Two lonely people, we were strangers in the night,
Up to the moment when we said our first hello,
Little did we know
That Love was just a glance away,
A warm embracing dance away...

Maybe our romantic relationship works because we are not always together. Maybe it's because at this stage of our lives, we are free of our earlier full-time responsibilities—raising children, paying the mortgage, and pleasing the in-laws. And maybe it's because—at this stage of our lives—companionship, dating, and romance are just plain fun. We both have our separate interests—Lew is an avid sports fan and champion golfer. I have my friendships, and love my fitness activities and my writing. But when we are together—almost like teenagers—our separate worlds simply disappear, and it's just the two of us.

Ever since that first night
We've been together
Lovers at first sight, in love forever
It turned out so right
For strangers in the night

EPILOGUE

It's been three years (or more than a thousand days) since I entered this new chapter in my life. Now that I have shared my personal journey with you, I am sure you can see that while we all may have the same title—widowhood—each and every one of us will handle our new challenges in different and perhaps rather unique ways.

I read somewhere that most things in life (like babies and seedlings) start off small and with time become bigger and perhaps even more wonderful.

But grief after death of a spouse is different. It starts off as an all-encompassing emotion, and then—with time—becomes diminished—but with hard work, it can become an opportunity for transformation.

I wrote this book as a way to share with others what I did to learn to live on my own. Perhaps from my experiences, other widows will gain courage and insight to help them move forward. We're sort of like a sorority - we pledge to help each other.

During these past three years, I learned to applauded my strengths and accept my shortcomings, as well to

113

discover how to be truly comfortable in my own skin.

I learned to feel relaxed and safe when alone in my house - as well as to pay the bills on time, know the difference between regular and preferred stocks, travel internationally and yes, to remember which days I needed to put the trash out at curbside.

Essentially, the more I managed to take care of what was needed, the better I felt about myself. And the more confidence I had, the more sure I became about all that I could—and should—do on my own. It was a slow process, but it helped me to gradually feel much calmer and a lot more at peace with myself.

There have been—and still are—some extremely sad moments when I miss Ed so terribly—mostly when it comes to anything regarding our children and grandchildren. But through the sadness and even some setbacks like spilling gasoline all over my new shoes the first time I pumped gas by myself or missed the deadline for paying my taxes, I still managed to experience the joyful feeling of a new love in my life.

Now—with my 80th birthday creeping ever close—I don't think about "tomorrows" anymore. Each day needs to be special—and maybe even better than the day before. And as long as I am healthy and mentally able, I've got whole lot of living to do!

ACKNOWLEDGMENTS

It only takes one person to put pen to paper, but I am the luckiest gal in the world to have had an assembly of caring people—a veritable village—to push my story forward.

First on my list is Marilyn Murray Willison, editor, friend, grammarian, disciplinarian, confidant, and cheerleader, who—when this book was just a tiny thought—grabbed me by my collar, and wouldn't let go until I made it to the finish line. Week in and week out—especially whenever I'd think, "Who would want to read about my journey?"—she would give me the courage to continue. In her words, "Your honesty will help so many other women. So keep writing!"

Thanks to my "big sister" Evelyn Grapek, and friends Ed Elkon, Myra Linker, Phyliss Napoli, Ann Bair, Barbara Pinkiert, who—at the drop of a hat—were always ready to listen to my first drafts as well as the rewrites, and who never got bored.

A shout out to the core members of my wonderful writing group, who gave me the courage to honestly express my innermost feelings for this personal widowhood memoir: Pat Williams, Lea Becker, Bunny Shulman, Joe Bernadino, Lee Ravine and Barbara Bixon. And, of course, thanks to Angela Shaw for her "Grace Under Pressure" typing skills.

And to my very special friend—Dr. Lewis Licht—who had more confidence in me, and in what I could accomplish than I had in myself. Lew's dogged determination and drive to get that "hole in one" was contagious and inspiring. He was my coach who cheered me forward in every loving, caring and supportive way.

And to my three wonderful, amazing daughters— Laurie, Jennifer and Kimberly—who always rolled their eyes whenever I would say, "Life is a journey." But this very honest book is proof that it really is! If nothing else, girls, I hope the words on these pages will provide the inspiration to remind you that no matter what painful issues you may face in your lives, you—and only you— can always decide to move forward.

When you girls were little, you frequently asked me to read and reread (ad nauseum) a little yellow book titled *The Little Train That Could.* The story is about a little train that had to take a heavy load of coal over to the other side of the mountain, which was an overwhelming job for a little train. But with the constant mantra "I think I can, I think I can " the little guy finally made it up to the top.

Girls, if I can move forward even when I don't think I can—so can you!